Gardening WITH THE EXPERTS

ANNUALS
& BIENNIALS

Gardening WITH THE EXPERTS

ANNUALS & BIENNIALS

HUGH REDGROVE

Bloomsbury Books
London

Front cover: **Phlox drummondii** in various shades.
Frontispiece: **Tagetes patula** French marigolds (orange and yellow),
Salvia splendens (scarlet), **Phlox drummondii** (pink) and **Lobularia maritima** (border).

Photographs: Kevin Burchett courtesy Weldon Trannies: page 26.
J. Filshie courtesy Weldon Trannies: page 11.
Ray Joyce courtesy of Weldon Trannies:
Pages 6, 7, 9, 10, 13, 14, 18 (below), 19, 20, 23, 24, 25, 27, 30, 33, 36, 37, 39, 42, 43, 46.
Tony Rodd courtesy of Weldon Trannies: page 41.
Weldon Trannies: front cover, frontispiece, pages 15, 45.

Published by Harlaxton Publishing Ltd
2 Avenue Road, Grantham, Lincolnshire, NG31 6TA, United Kingdom.
A Member of the Weldon International Group of Companies.

First published in 1990 (Limp)
Reprint 1991 (Cased)
Reprint 1992 (Cased)

© Copyright Harlaxton Publishing Ltd
© Copyright design Harlaxton Publishing Ltd

This edition published in 1993 by
Bloomsbury Books
an imprint of
The Godfrey Cave Group
42 Bloomsbury Street, London. WC1B 3QJ
under license from Harlaxton Publishing Ltd.

Publishing Manager: Robin Burgess
Illustrations: Kathie Baxter Smith
Typeset in UK by Seller's, Grantham
Produced in Singapore by Imago

British Library Cataloguing-in-Publication data.
A catalogue record for this book is available from the British Library.
Title: Gardening with the Experts: Annuals & Biennials.
ISBN:1 85471 171 7

CONTENTS

INTRODUCTION

True annuals are plants that will complete their life cycle within twelve months of sowing. Biennials require two growing seasons to do so and are usually sown in summer to flower in the following spring and summer.

Many other plants that botanists would define as perennial can be treated as annuals, although some are described as half-hardy and, while able to flower well in their first season, are not hardy enough to be used for more than one year. An example is the brilliant scarlet *Salvia splendens*. Half-hardy annuals are usually raised in a greenhouse, then pricked out (transplanted into larger boxes) a few centimetres apart and grown under protection, before being planted out.

Above: **Aster chinensis** *(Callistephus) are half-hardy annuals grown from cuttings or seed.*
Page opposite: **Salvia splendens**, *a popular half-hardy annual.*

BIENNIALS

The winter hardiness of the biennial group depends on the district in which they are grown, local advice must be sought in cases such as *Begonia semperflorens*, *Browallia* and *Primula malacoïdes*, etc. But there are significant advantages in planting out in late summer or autumn for all those hardy enough to winter well. For example, Canterbury bells (*Campanula medium*) that are planted outside as transplants in autumn will flower well the following summer, but if planted out in spring they will usually flower twelve months later! Sweet Williams behave in a similar way.

Biennials are usually sown in a seedbed in the open, or in boxes in a frame or greenhouse to be transplanted as seedlings, and put in their final quarters in late autumn, as in the case of wallflowers (*Cheiranthus cheiri*), which are best in cool

*Above: Dwarf **cinerarias** are suitable for shady spots.*
*Page opposite: **Primula malacoïdes** comes in white, pink and red shades.*

regions, and double daisies (*Bellis*). With forget-me-nots (*Myosotis*) and *Cinerarias* it is quite important to plant out in autumn, as these flower early and therefore need planting out well ahead of flowering time.

Cinerarias are suitable only for areas free from frost, but in such areas they are very showy and especially useful for shady gardens. There are short, medium and tall types and the colour range is wide. Especially good are the rich blue shades.

Some of those which are not frost hardy include *Begonia semperflorens*, *Coleus* grown for foliage colour, *Dahlias* which have perennial tubers and *Impatiens*. *Impatiens* has become a very popular plant, available in both short and taller varieties, and in numerous double-flowered cultivars. The

*Double **Impatiens** cultivars are available in several colours.*

latter are mainly propagated by cuttings. They grow well in full sun if watered, or in shade, and are very popular container plants for patios.

*Above: **Rudbeckia hirta tetra** 'Gloriosa' are available in single and double-flowered varieties. Page opposite: Foxgloves (**Digitalis**) can be grown in semi-shade.*

HARDY BIENNIALS

These are plants that are sown the year before they are expected to flower. They are raised in a seedbed outdoors or in a cool, shady frame and may be thinned out or transplanted when large enough. Planting out should be done in autumn for best results. If buying from your garden centre in punnets or seedling trays, be in early. Even where winters are mild, planting at that time results in smaller flowering plants, except perhaps with pansies and violas.

Some popular hardy biennials are:

O Sun   ◑ Partial shade   ● Shade

Name and colours	Height in cm.	Sun or Shade	Sow outdoors	Sow in boxes	Time of sowing	Remarks
Bellis (double daisy) various colours.	15	O ◑	X		Summer/ Autumn	Transplant.
Browallia 'Jingle Bells'; mixed colours, bright blue.	40	◑	X		Autumn/ Spring	Transplant. Warm regions.
Campanula medium (Canterbury bells)	30-60	O ◑		X	Summer	Transplant.
Cheiranthus allionii; bright orange.	30	O	X		Autumn	Cool regions
Cheiranthus cheiri (wallflower); gold, primrose, orange, red.	40	O	X	X	Autumn	Cool regions
Dianthus barbatus (Sweet William); salmon.	30	O ◑	X	X	Summer	Often perennial.
Digitalis (foxglove); cream, pink, purple.	100	O	X	X	Summer/ Autumn	
Lunaria (honesty); white, purple.	75	O ◑	X		Summer	Silverpods Difficult to transplant.
Mattiola (stock 'Brompton') range of colours	35	O		X	Summer	Scented
Myosotis (forget-me-not); blue, white.	15-20	O ◑	X		Summer/ Autumn	

Name and colours	Height in cm.	Sun or Shade	Sow outdoors	Sow in boxes	Time of sowing	Remarks
Pansy and viola;	15-20	O ◑	X	X	Summer/ Autumn	Pansies dark blotches. Violas coloured.
Primula malacoïdes; white, pink, crimson.	40	O ◑		X	Summer	Warm regions.
Primula obconica; white, blue, pink, red, salmon.	35	O ◑		X	Summer	Warm regions.
Primula vulgaris elatior (Polyanthus); white, pink, yellow to crimson.	15-25	O ◑		X	Autumn/ Summer	perennial or biennial
Rudbeckia hirta gloriosa; (black-eyed-Susan) yellow, orange, bronze.	45-90	O		X	Autumn	Long lasting flowers. single & double
Verbena; bright colours	30	O	X	X	Spring	Spreading.

Stocks *are alwaysa mixture of single and double flowers.*

ANNUALS

Easy to grow Annuals

Those annuals that can be sown directly onto well-prepared beds in the garden and will come quickly into flower are bound to be popular if they are capable of sustaining flowering for a lengthy period, and there are numerous suitable varieties. In a few cases they must be sown in situ, but in most cases (unless otherwise noted) they may be sown in boxes and transplanted — an arrangement that permits a faster succession of bloom after early-flowering annuals or bulbs have finished.

Before sowing time, the growing sites should be prepared. Compost should be worked in, and planting mix may be applied to the surface if the soil is very lumpy and heavy. Then choose a dry day, apply a little general fertiliser and rake it in. Seed can be broadcast or it can be sown in shallow drills about 8 cm apart. If sowing is in drills, it will be possible to keep down the seedling weed with a small hand hoe, which is quicker than hand-weeding. The seed rows should be covered with soil, or the seed raked in if broadcast. After germination, some thinning may be necessary.

Some seedlings may be safely transplanted, but the following do not transplant easily: *Clarkia, Eschscholzia, Godetia, Gypsophila, Linaria, Linum 'Rubrum', Nigella, Phlox drummondii* and poppies.

Remember that if annuals need staking it is far, far better to support them with twiggy stakes while they are still erect, and that the removal of spent flowers will prolong flowering and improve the plant's appearance.

The following table provides a selection of popular hardy annuals.

Above: **Phlox drummondii** *seedlings do not transplant well.*
Page opposite: **Chrysanthemums** *are available in a wide range of colours.*

O Sun   ◑ Partial shade   ● Shade

Name and colours	Height in cm.	Sun or Shade	Sow outdoors	Sow in boxes	Time of sowing	Remarks
Lobularia maritima; white, rose, purple.	15	O◑	X		Spring or at any time	Often self seeds
Calendula (marigold); yellow, orange, red.	30-45	O	X	X	Summer/ Autumn	
Clarkia elegans; double mixed, white, pink shades.	60	O	X		Spring	Sow in situ
Cleome (spider flower); pink, mauve, white.	90	O		X	Spring	
Cornflower; white, pink, red, blue.	25-90	O◑	X	X	Autumn	Cool regions
Cosmos, daisy-like; white, pink, crimson.	90	O	X		Spring	
Delphinium 'Imperial Double' ; white, salmon, pink, red	120	O	X	X	Autumn	Cool regions only.
Dimorphotheca, daisy-like; pink, white, yellow.	10-20	O	X		Spring	Light soil
Eschscholzia; wide colour range.	30	O	X		Spring	Sow in situ
Godetia azaleaflora; mixed.	40	O	X		Spring	Sow in situ
Godetia 'Sybil Sherwood'; double salmon-edged white	45	O	X		Spring	Sow in situ
Gypsophila; white, rose.	40-45	O	X		Spring	Sow in situ
Helichrysum; wide colour range.	75	O	X	X	Spring	Sow in situ
Helipterum roseum; double mixed, white and rose.		30	O	X		Spring
Iberis (Candytuft) 'Fairy Mixed' or 'Giant White'	20-30	O	X	X	Autumn	

Name and colours	Height in cm.	Sun or Shade	Sow outdoors	Sow in boxes	Time of sowing	Remarks
Lathyrus vernus (Sweet pea); 'Bijou Dwarf' many colours.	30	O	X	X	Autumn/ Spring	No stakes required
Lathyrus odoratus (Sweet pea); climbing many colours.	175	O	X	X	Autumn/ early Spring	Scented
Lavatera (mallow); white, pink, rose.	60-90	O	X	X	Winter/ Spring	
Limnanthes douglasii; white, yellow.	15	O		X	Spring	
Limonium sinuataum; white, blue, pink, yellow.	45	O	X	X	Spring	Sow early in boxes
Limonium suworowii; pink spikes.	70	O	X		Spring	Sow early in boxes
Linaria (toadflax); various colours.	22	O	X		Spring	Sow in Situ
Linum 'Rubrum'; (red annual flax)	30	O	X		Spring	Sow in situ
Lychnis viscaria; mixed white, pink, red, blue.	30	O	X		Spring	
Nigella damascena (love-in-a-mist); rose, blue, white.	35	O	X		Spring	Sow in situ
Papaver (Poppy) 'Shirley'; wide colour range.	60	O	X		Spring	Sow in situ
Resida Mignonette 'Machet Rubin'; reddish colours.	40	O	X		Spring	Sow in situ
Scabiosa; white, pink, red, blue.	45-90	O	X	X	Spring	

Above: **Papaver** *(Poppies) should be sown in situ.*
Below: Sweet marigolds **(Calendula)** *require full sun.*

Above: **Cleome spinosa** *grows almost a metre tall.*
Below: **Lychnis viscaria** *is an easily grown annual.*

Half-hardy Annuals

These are the kinds of annuals that must be raised in a frame or greenhouse, or in a few cases sown outdoors after the danger of frost has passed. The majority, however, are more easily raised in a greenhouse.

Germination time will vary, and most kinds require pricking out into boxes or pots of potting compost. If you wish to avoid this chore, you can use small peat pots and sow a few seeds in each one.

Once the plants are strong enough and have been hardened off (allowing a gradual lowering of the temperature), they can be transplanted intact, pot and all, to their flowering positions. Some of the seeds are very small, such as those of *Lobelia*, *begonias* and *petunias*. These need careful sowing, quite thinly, with little or no soil covering. They must not be allowed to dry out, even on the surface, and large, clear plastic bags can be used to enclose the pots but must be removed as soon as germination is complete. Keep them out of direct sunlight.

Nowadays the numerous garden centres will often do all this work for you, offering a good range of these plants in punnets ready for planting out, but it may well be that you have seed that you have collected in your own garden, or perhaps you have found some varieties unavailable in punnets. In any case, you will find that raising your own seedlings can add a great deal of interest to your gardening.

You will also realise how inexpensive the seedlings at the garden centre really are!

The following are are selection of popular half-hardy annuals:

Amaranthus 'Molten Torch' is a half-hardy annual in warm regions.

ANNUALS

○ Sun   ◑ Partial shade   ● Shade

Name and colours	Height in cm.	Sun or Shade	Sow outdoors	Sow in boxes	Time of sowing	Remarks
Ageratum; blue, pink.	20	○◑	X	X	Spring	Avoid frost
Amaranthus caudatus; (love lies-bleeding) red spikes.	50	○	X	X	Spring	
Antirrhinum (snapdragon); tall, intermedlate, dwarf many colours.	35-75	○◑		X	Winter/ Spring	Cool site in warm regions.
Aster; single, double, many colours.	22-60	○◑	X	X	Spring	Stake tall varieties.
Begonia, bedding; white, pink, scarlet.	15-30	○◑		X	Spring	Sow thinly.
Dianthus caryophyllus (Carnation) —'Giant Chaubaud' mixed colours. —'Marguerite'; mixed colours.	45	○		X	Autumn	Transplant.
Chrysanthemum 'Korean Rainbow'; wide range of colours.	60-80	○		X	Spring/ Autumn	Transplant.
Cineraria; blue, white, purple, crlmson.	20-60	◑●	X	X	Autumn	Frost tender Good in pots
Coleus; wide range of foliage colour.	20-90	○◑		X	Spring	Frost tender.
Euphorbia marginata (snow-on-the-mountain); foliage green and white.	60	○		X	Spring	
Geranium 'Summe Showers'; good colour range.	30	○		X	Winter	Trailing habit.
Impatiens; various colours.	15-30	○◑		X	Spring	Also double & bicolour Frost tender.

○ Sun   ◑ Partial shade   ● Shade

Name and colours	Height in cm.	Sun or Shade	Sow outdoors	Sow in boxes	Time of sowing	Remarks
Lobelia erinus; blue, pink, white.	20	O		X	Spring	Sow thinly
Lobelia erinus pendula; blue shades.	15-30	O		X	Spring	Sow thinly Trailing habit
Mesembryanthemum criniflorum (Livingstone daisy) buff, apricot, crimson, pink.	8	O	X	X	Spring	Prefers dry soil.
Nemesia 'Carnival'; mixed, all colours.	22	O	X	X	Autumn/ Spring	
Nicotiana (tobacco plant); white, green red, pink.	22-90	O	X	X	Spring	
Petunia 'Cascade'; —very large single, mixed	30	O		X	Spring	Sow thinly suits planters & baskets
—very large double all colours.	30	O		X	Spring	Sow thinly compact habit
—'Color Parade', mixed.	60	O		X	Spring	Sow thinly Transplant when small.
Phlox drummondii; mixed, wide range of colours.	20-35	O	X	X	Autumn/ Spring	Does not transplant well
Portulaca; mixed.	15	O	X	X	Spring	Usually semi-double
Salvia farinacea 'Victoria'; violet blue spikes.	45	O		X	Spring	Long-lasting
Salvia splendens; scarlet, pink, white, purple.	30-45	O		X	Spring	Scarlet is best known.
Tagetes 'Gem'; lemon, orange.	15	O		X	Spring	Single; fine laced foliage.

Name and colours	Height in cm.	Sun or Shade	Sow outdoors	Sow in boxes	Time of sowing	Remarks
Tagetes erecta, Marigold, African; primrose, gold, orange.	20-35	O		X	Spring	Usually double flowers
Tagetes erecta. Marigold, French; lemon, gold, orange, brown.	15-20	O		X	Spring	
Zinnia elgans; mixed, wide range of colours.	60	O		X	Spring	Transplant
—'Envy'; chartreuse green.	75	O		X	Spring	Plant after frost
—'Giant Dahlia'; mixed.	75	O		X	Spring	Plant after frost

Zinnias are very showy and long-lasting.

Above: Annuals are often planted as cottage borders.
*Below: This tobacco plant (**Nicotiana**) is lime-green.*

Above: **Petunias** *should be grown in a sunny position.*
Below: **Begonia** *trails at a Botanic Garden.*

ANNUALS AND BIENNIALS FOR THE GREENHOUSE

Many annuals and biennials may be grown to flower in winter, or earlier in the spring than they would develop outdoors. At low cost they will augment other decorative plants and bulbs.

If the greenhouse can be moderately heated in the winter, the range of suitable plants will be wider, especially in those areas where frosts are heavier than just a few degrees below zero. Close attention will need to be paid to watering and ventilation of these plants, the amount of care will vary according to the local climate and the maximum light available in winter, to avoid lanky growth.

FOR UNHEATED GREENHOUSES

Anchusa 'Blue Angel': long sprays; rich, deep blue; 25 cm; sow in spring.
Antirrhinum: various colours and heights; dwarf varieties for pot culture; sow in late

Primula vulgaris (*Primroses*) *can be grown in greenhouses.*

26

Primula malacoïdes 'Redgrove Pink' is suitable for frost-free greenhouses.

winter or early spring.

Calendula 'Fiesta': dwarf; yellow and orange; 30 cm; sow in summer/autumn.

Centaurea (Cornflower)'Baby Blue': bushy; rich, deep blue; 25 cm; sow in autumn.

Godetia 'Salmon Prince': pink overlaid with orange; 30 cm; sow in spring.

Delphinium (Larkspur), dwarf hyacinth flowered: mixed; 30 cm.

Lathyrus (Sweet pea) 'Bijou Dwarf': mixed; 30 cm; sow in autumn.

Petunia 'Cascade': large single; various colours; 30 cm; superb for tubs and hanging baskets; sow in spring.

Primula vulgaris elatior (Polyanthus) 'Crescendo': superb mixture; 15-20 cm; shade in summer; sow late autumn.

Primula vulgaris (Primrose) 'Spectrum Mixed': fine colour range; 15 cm; shade in summer; sow late autumn.

Malcolmia maritima (Stock) 'East Lothian': compact; mixed colours; 45 cm; cool regions; sow in early autumn.

Tagetes (Marigold) 'Red Cherry': bright orange red; 30 cm; well suited to pots; sow in autumn.

*Overleaf: The **Begonia** Conservatory at Ballarat Botanic Gardens.*

FOR FROST-FREE GREENHOUSES

Begonia semperflorens: white, pink, rose, scarlet; 15-30 cm; sow in spring.
Browallia 'Jingle Bells': 5 cm flowers; many shades; 40 cm; sow in autumn/ spring.
Calceolaria 'Mixed Colours': yellow to red; 25 cm; sow in summer.
Chrysanthemum 'Charm Mixed': 40-50 cm; suitable for pots; sow in spring.
Cineraria: dwarf; various colours; 20 cm; sow in summer.
Coleus 'Rainbow Mixed': for foliage colour; 30-50 cm; sow in spring.
Impatiens 'Accent Strain': many colours; dwarf 15 cm; sow in spring.
Primula malacoïdes: white, pink, red; 40 cm; flowers in August; sow in summer.
Primula obconica: white, blue, pink, salmon, red; 35 cm; sow in summer.
Schizanthus 'Star Parade': compact; multi-coloured; 45 cm; sow in summer.

Chrysanthemums 'Charm' *are easily grown from seed.*

ANNUALS AND BIENNIALS FOR SEMI-SHADE

Very few annuals or biennials, if any, will grow in dense shade, particularly under evergreen trees. In positions of part-shade where the soil is moderately fertile and there will be some sun for part of the day, some annuals will give a reasonable display.

Ageratum: blue, pink; 20 cm; sow in spring.

Anchusa 'Blue Angel': deep blue; 25 cm; sow in spring.

Begonia semperflorens, bedding: white, pink, red; 15-25 cm; sow in seed trays.

Bellis (double daisy): various colours; 15 cm; sow in summer/autumn.

Browallia 'Jingle Bells': mixed colours; 40 cm; sow in autumn/spring.

Campanula medium (Canterbury bells): blue, pink, white; 30-60 cm; sow under glass in late spring and plant early summer.

Lobelia: blue, buff, apricot, crimson, pink, white; 15 cm; sow thinly in trays in spring.

Lobularia maritima: white, pink, purple; 15 cm; sow at any time.

Violas *can be grown in partial shade.*

Mimulus: mixed, orange and yellow; 20 cm; prefers moist soil; sow in seed trays.

Myosotis (forget-me-not): blue shades, white; 15-20 cm; sow in summer/ autumn.

Nicotiana (tobacco plant): white, pink, red, green; 22-90 cm; sow in spring.

Nigella damascena (love-in-a-mist): white, blue, pink shades; 35 cm; sow in situ in early spring.

Viola x *Wittrockiana* (Pansy) and *viola*: various colours, especially Fl Hybrids; 15-20 cm; sow summer/early autumn.

Phlox drummondii: mixed, wide colour range; 20-35 cm; sow autumn/spring.

Above: **Viola** x **wittrockiana** (Pansies) *are popular edging plants.*
Page opposite: **Lobelia** *'Flamingo' is a pink cultivar.*

32

ANNUALS AND BIENNIALS IN HANGING BASKETS

Hanging baskets provide a simple and very attractive way of decorating a porch or terrace during the summer, and annuals and biennials can play an important part. They may also be used in the greenhouse.

Baskets of various sizes are usually made from stout galvanised wire. Others are made from plastic mesh. Each basket should first be lined with sphagnum moss.

Alternatively, polythene can be used as a lining, with holes punched in the base for drainage. For larger baskets it is possible to combine these two linings, which can reduce watering while retaining a good appearance.

The soil should be a good potting compost with the addition of a slow action fertiliser. Planting should be with well-

Geraniums look attractive in hanging baskets.

established plants just coming into flower. Put the larger plants into place first and then smaller plants such as trailing *Lobelia* and *Alyssum* can be tucked in between. *Geraniums*, both the erect 'zonal' types and the 'trailing' ivy-leaf types, are popular long-flowering plants, and the following annuals and biennials are also suitable: *Ageratum, Begonia semperflorens, Browallia, Gypsophila, Nemesia,* petunias (especially the 'Cascade' varieties), trailing *Lobelia*, trailing *Nasturtiums* and *Verbena*. Trailing *nasturtiums* can be used by pushing seeds into rhe soil at planting time.

During the warm weather one must be prepared to water the basket every day, but there are watering nozzles available which are designed to avoid having to bring the basket down for watering. After watering, hanging baskets are very heavy, so make sure that they are hung from strong hooks.

They should be placed in positions where they do not get full sun during the hottest part of the day, but where they are not in deep shade.

ANNUALS AND BIENNIALS FOR EVERLASTING FLOWERS

There are a number of suitable annuals and biennials that are ideal for drying. They will also add colour to mixed borders while growing, then to indoor winter decoration. Some have interesting seed pods which may be dried for similar purposes.

Unless otherwise stated, these seeds are usually sown under glass, allowing about six weeks for development before they are planted out, but it is also possible, in warm regions on light soils, to sow the seeds direct in sunny positions and thin them out as required.

The flower stems should generally be cut just before the flowers are fully developed, tied in small bunches and hung upside down in a warm airy place under cover.
Helipterum roseum: mixed, white, pink, rose; large-flowered; 45 cm.
Helichrysum bracteatum 'Monstrosum':

Above: The delicate white flowers of Queen Anne's Lace.
Page opposite: **Lunaria variegata** *has silvery seed pods which are good for drying.*

HANG EVERLASTING FLOWERS
IN SMALL BUNCHES.

white, pink, yellow, crimson; double daisies with incurving petals; tall to 90 cm; dwarf 30 cm; always cut in bud for drying.

Lunaria (honesty): white, purple flowers; silvery seed pods; 75 cm.
Molucella laevis (bells of Ireland): green flower bracts on graceful stems turning straw-coloured when dried; 70 cm.
Nigella damascena (love-in-a-mist): rose, blue, white; inflated seed capsules; 35 cm.
Limonium sinuatum: white, yellow, blue, rose; flat flower heads; to 45 cm; plant out on light soils in autumn.
Limonium suworowii (pink rats' tails): delightful, graceful pink spikes to 70 cm; sow in early spring. There are several perennial varieties of Statice (Limonium).
Xeranthemum annuum: white, pink, mauve, purple; easy to grow; 45 cm.

CLIMBING ANNUALS

There are a number of climbers that are rapid growers, ideal for quickly covering fences, trellises, walls or tree stumps.

Sweet peas and scarlet runner beans are favourites, and these need sites that have been well prepared by deep digging and the addition of good compost or well rotted animal manure.

It is usually necessary to provide netting (either plastic or wire) which is stretched out, or wound around a tree stump. To brighten up a hedge, climbing *nasturtiums* may be sown in situ, but hedge-cutting will have to wait until the winter.

The tender climbers—half-hardy annuals (HHA) and half-hardy perennials (HHP), should be sown under glass and planted out when frosts are over. The others—hardy annuals (HA)—can be sown outside in early spring.

Cobaea scandens (cathedral bells): HHA; large violet-blue bells.
Geranium 'Summer Showers': HHA; pink and red shades.
Ipomoea (morning glory) 'Heavenly Blue': HHA, sky blue.
Lathyrus (sweet pea): HA; climbing forms; many colours.
Maurandia erubescens: HHA; rosy carmine trumpets, hairy leaves.
Thunbergia alata (black-eyed Susan): HHA

or HP; type form is orange, but mixed colours with black eye are now available.
Tropaeolum canariense (canary creeper): HA; yellow flowers.

Maurandia erubescens
is a fast-growing climber.

ANNUALS FOR THE ROCK GARDEN

Annuals are out of place in a rock garden unless they are very small. However, if carefully chosen they will provide colour at a season when few other plants are blooming. Those listed may be sown direct or raised in boxes for transplanting. They are, of course, equally suitable for troughs, border-edging and small beds.

Anchusa 'Blue Angel': deep blue; compact and shade tolerant; 25 cm.

Iberis (candytuft) 'Fairy Mixed': white, rose, purple, 20 cm.

Linaria 'Fairy Bouquet': all colours in mixture; 22 cm.

Lobularia maritima: white, pink, violet; easy to grow; 20 cm.

Mesembryanthemum criniflorum(Livingstone daisy): buff, apricot, crimson, pink shades; 8 cm; full sun.

Nemophila menziessii 'Baby Blue Eyes': sky blue with white centres; 20 cm.

Small annuals in a rock garden.

ANNUALS
TO FOLLOW BULBS

By the time spring-flowering bulbs have finished blooming and the foliage has died down, it is becoming late to sow for summer flowers and so in many cases plants previously raised in punnets or boxes would be the best choice.

Refer to "Half-hardy Annuals" for ideas on suitable plants. However, there are a number of colourful varieties that can be sown as late as mid-winter with success.

Most varieties listed under "Annuals for the Rock Garden" are suitable, but the following are taller and may be preferred.
Dimorphotheca aurantiaca (star of the veldt) white, yellow, salmon; daisy-like; 15 cm.
Eschscholzia: single mixed or double art shades; 30 cm.
Phlox drummondii: brilliant mixed colours; 20-35 cm.

These plants prefer sunny situations.

*These yellow **petunias** are half-hardy annuals.*

F1 HYBRIDS

Hybrid seeds have become very important in horticulture and will be increasingly so in the future. They are produced by breeding from two selected parents with special qualities which are usually combined in the offspring. Seed from the first cross is normally called F1 Hybrid.

The production of this seed is time-consuming and costly, and because further generations are very variable or in some cases there is no germination at all, it is necessary to repeat the same cross year after year.

The advantages are often considerable: a quicker and more even germination, extra vigour producing higher yields, a greater resistance to pests and diseases, greatly increased periods of blooming and larger flowers. Many new strains of F1 petunias, *Begonia semperflorens*, *Ageratum* and African marigolds are all flowers that have been transformed in recent years. Toma-

Dianthus *'Bravo', an attractive hybrid.*

*This **begonia** 'multiflora' is available in several colours.*

toes, sweet corn, brussels sprouts and cabbages are vegetables which have been greatly improved.

The most exciting of the recent introductions is the multiflora type of 'zonal' *geranium* which blooms from seed sixteen to twenty weeks after sowing. The 'Carefree' and 'Pinto' strains are available in separate colours and are often on sale at garden centres from midsummer onwards. They are very bushy, with at least two heads of bloom at the time of purchase. Home gardeners will probably prefer to buy the plants, for they need warm greenhouse temperatures (22° to 23°C) to germinate freely.

GROWING SWEET PEAS

Lathyrus odoratus is the plant we all know as the sweet pea and it is among the most attractive, prolific and sweet-smelling of all the annuals.

There are clubs and societies entirely devoted to the cultivation of sweet peas, probably the only annual to have achieved such popularity. Since their introduction to Britain from Sicily in 1699, the original small purple flower has been transformed into the wonderful range of large-flowered, multicoloured varieties available today. In the process most of the rather elusive scent has been retained. Now we have dwarf strains to suit the small garden, which do not need staking.

Those who grow for exhibition go to great lengths to achieve perfection, starting with site preparation by digging a trench to two spits deep (spade depths) and incorporating much well-rotted animal manure. Good results can be obtained with rather less effort, so long as a fertile, well-drained site is chosen, with plenty of humus in the form of compost or manure and in full sun.

Provide support for the usual climbing types in the form of netting firmly fixed to uprights. For exhibition flowers with long stems, sweet peas are sometimes grown as cordons with side shoots removed to allow a single stem to develop, or perhaps two.

However, most growers will allow their plants to branch freely after pinching out

the main shoot at about 30 cm.

Although it is quite satisfactory to sow the seed direct into prepared soil outdoors in autumn or early spring, most people prefer to sow into trays of potting mix or into pots. Peat pots are very suitable, for the undisturbed root system may then be planted out intact.

The seed is sometimes hard-coated, if so, they should be chipped with the aid of a sharp knife or soaked in water for twenty-four hours before sowing.

Sweet peas are also susceptible to fungus diseases in the soil so it is advisable to plant in a different place each year. If this is not possible, it may be necessary to sterilise the soil with Basamid. This would require a delay of about six weeks before planting out.

While sweet peas are usually grown in straight rows as for vegetables, some people grow them in circular groups and this type of informal planting is much preferred for a mixed border. Arrange a circle of 2 metre bamboo canes with a diameter of about 60 cm, encircle it with netting, plant your sweet peas about 20 cm apart around the netting and in due course you should have a beautiful pillar of sweet pea blooms.

Picking all the faded blooms once a week will prolong flowering. When the plants have finished flowering, cut them off at ground level. In common with other

Sweet peas require rich, well-drained soil.

members of the pea and bean varieties, the roots grow nodules that have a high nitrogen content, if they are left to rot in the soil they will be a benefit to next crop.

You can obtain tall-growing sweet peas seeds under various names or in separate colours, in most cases they will have at least five flowers on each stem. These are the best for general cultivation.

There are intermediate strains, such as the 'Snooper', which has dark green foliage without tendrils or wavy flowers. Smaller still, is the 'Bijou Dwarf' strain which grows 30 to 40 cm high, has a rich colour mixture of rufffled flowers with stems long enough to pick. It is ideal for the very small garden.

Some distinctive sweet peas called 'Two Tone' have been bred in New Zealand by Dr Keith Hammett. Each flower is bicoloured, the standards being a different colour from the wings. They are best sown in early spring since they are summer-flowering. Plant them in full sun, as they require eleven to twelve hours of daylight to flower. Their colours include combinations of rose, white, pink, lavender as well as navy.

To prolong the vase life of sweet peas, pick them before they are fully open; burn the stems in a flame or plunge them into boiling water for a few minutes then stand them up to their necks in cold water.

*Overleaf; New Guinea **Impatiens** needs warm growing conditions.*

INDEX

The page numbers in **bold** type indicate illustrations.